This Book is easy enough for the "First Time Repairer",
yet detailed enough to teach the most experienced
Technician...

The Tools Used For The GPU Reflow Process

Hand Tools Used
Screwdriver: you will need both micro sized screwdrivers and medium sized ones, it is best to find a variety pack so that you will get ones with different shaped tips, being narrow ones and blunt ones.

Pliers: the needle-nosed pliers are the most used, and not the typical thick ones available, you will need to search out thin and narrow ones, the smaller the better as you will need to use these pliers in very tight spaces and picking up very small items.

Plastic Pry Tools: This will include guitar picks, plastic wand style pry tool (like the ones given with iPod repair part purchases), thin plastic cards and similar.

Toothbrush: Used quite often, it will allow the removal of dust and debris without harming the components.

Power Tools Used

Heat Gun/Hot Air gun: This will be used in the reflow process for the video chip connection. You can purchase these at any Home Improvement store all over the world, they are typically used in the Painting field, they are used to strip paint. In Electronics repair they are used as well, just not advertised as such. You will need on that can reach solder melting point temperatures. The 2 setting (high-low) Heat guns will suffice, though I do recommend the multi setting 600 to 1200 watt heat gun, set to 700-800 on the heat dial.

Thermometer: The recommended thermometer is an infrared laser guided digital thermometer; you must ensure that it can read temperatures past 223 degrees Celsius and 433 degrees Fahrenheit.

Reflowing the GPU

All the Problems described are Graphics Related

Faulty Nvidia Chip, Both Intel And AMD Based Motherboards, Though More Common on the AMD..

The symptoms of the Laptop Powering on and Shutting Off Repeatedly, Or, Powering On and Having No Video...

Or... Power Strip Lights Up, Beeps, Shuts Down...Or, No Power At All, Or, Intermittent Loss Of Wireless/Video

Goes In And Out/Touchpad Slows and Freezes

To Fix this issue, You will need to Reflow The Graphics Chip.

About the BGA
The BGA is descended from the pin grid array (PGA), which is a package with one face covered (or partly covered) with pins in a grid pattern. These pins conduct electrical signals from the integrated circuit to the printed circuit board (PCB) on which it is placed. In a BGA, the pins are replaced by balls of solder stuck to the bottom of the package. These solder spheres can be placed manually or with automated

equipment. The solder spheres are held in place with a tacky flux until soldering occurs. [1] The device is placed on a PCB that carries copper pads in a pattern that matches the solder balls. The assembly is then heated, either in a reflow oven or by an infrared heater, causing the solder balls to melt. Surface tension causes the molten solder to hold the package in alignment with the circuit board, at the correct separation distance, while the solder cools and solidifies.

Removing the Chip Sealant
A Thing To Look Out For...
Hewlett Packard is notorious for using the RED epoxy around the edge of the Graphics chip.. this epoxy is used to help secure the chip to the motherboard...
This is a process that is Hand Done at the Factory..
And Some Boards Will Have Only A Little Amount of this, Some Will Have Alot of it...And Some are Only Done On The Corner Edges....
If There Is Alot of This On Your Chip, You Might End Up Needing To Carefully (REAL CAREFULLY) Remove as much of this epoxy as able to.

HOW TO REMOVE THE RED (or clear) GPU/GRAPHICS CHIP SEALANT SAFELY FROM THE CHIPS OUTER EDGE:

You will need to prepare the board, covering any plastic parts, covering RAM ports, Covering CPU Base, etc....

Then Heat the Chips outer edge using The Heat Gun at 700 Degrees, Monitor the temperature with the infrared thermometer and bring the chips outer edge to a temperature of 145 degrees Celsius...

Reflowing the GPU
Video Failure Repairing, Video Chip/GPU/Graphics Chip Reflow-Repair Method
Do It Yourself Video Chip BGA Rework (Reflow)
Understanding the GPU, CPU, Memory Chips and Ball Grid Arrays (BGA's):
Q: What are these chip packages that Microsoft® calls the GPU, the CPU, and the Memory Chips? And why do they look so different from other components?

A: These are electronic chips that are packaged in what are called Ball Grid Array formats (BGA's). They are a relatively new form of Surface Mount Devices (SMD) and are similar to other components in that they have an integrated circuit (die) within the package and that they have connections to be Soldered. However, instead of leads at the side of the chip, the connections are balls underneath the chip): Faulty NVidia Chip...Both Intel and AMD Based Motherboards...Though More Common on the AMD... The symptoms of the Laptop Powering on and shutting off repeatedly...Or... Powering On and Having No Video...
Or... Power Strip Lights Up, Beeps, Shuts Down...Or...No Power At All...Or... Intermittent Loss

Of Wireless/Video Goes In And Out/Touchpad Slows and Freezes…

Next step Is preparing the Motherboard...you need to Insulate all areas around the Video Chip/GPU...This is where you will use the Tin Foil...make sure to Use About 4 Fold Thickness (fold the aluminum foil 4 times to make it thicker).. And Place Foil Over The CPU, Over Any Plastic Plug Ports... Over Any Capacitors Nearby...

It Is Important To Clear Your Work Area Now... You Will Be Working with A lot Of Heat and anything around will Get Real Hot

I Use Metal And Aluminum Foil, I also Work On A Marble Table, You Will Want To Make Sure That You Have Foil Or Non-Flammable Surface Under The Motherboard. The More You Cover... The Better

Now It's Time To Weight The Chip...This Serves 2 Purposes...

1.)   Most Graphics Chips Have An Epoxy That Goes Around The Edge Of The Chip To Hold It In Its Position And To Prevent Chip Rising and I explain in this book How to remove it safely...The Weight of the Coin Stack Helps To Get A Better Reflow...Don't Worry, It's Not Enough Weight To Squish The Chip Into The Board.. Through Trial And Error, I've Determined That 6 Quarters and 2 Nickels Is the Proper Weight for an NVidia Chip...Use Less Weight for a Smaller Chip.

2.)   The Stack of Quarters Also Helps to Spread the Heat More evenly and Helps Prevent the Upper Chip That Rests on the Video Chip from Overheating

Different Ways to Heat the Chip:
Rework Stations are common to Reflowing and Reballing IC Chipsets, They are machines that will brace the motherboard, allow for proper heating of the board before reflowing, to prevent board shock, they can concentrate the high heat to center on the IC chip needed to be reflowed without overheating other components… There are Hot Air Rework Stations, and there are Infrared Rework Stations… IR stations will heat the board using light… and can be known for yielding better results because the heat can be concentrated on the specific area without heating surrounding components.

You will be using Hot Air for your repairing… There are a lot of skeptics out there claiming that hot air methods Do Not work. This misinformation is wrong….In my opinion, it is a better option, specifically referring to the Use of a Hot Air Heat Gun. Reason being, you are able to maneuver the source of heat, and manipulate the Flow of heat by the use of Heat Gun Add-On Tips.

These add-on tips are extremely useful… You can purchase the exact tip needed to fit exactly over the chip needed to be reflowed… there are many different styles available.
Free movement of the heat source allows you to angle the hot air flow to reach under the chips edge better…You can adjust the Heat temperature on most Heat Guns..
You can also Use the 2 setting Heat guns, but you should practice Chip heating on a Non-Working motherboard to get used to the time length of chip heating.

Using a Hot Air gun together with an Infrared Digital Thermometer will yield just as accurate if not, more accurate results when reflowing (not referring to Reballing here), because you have the ability to angle the heat source, and the ability to circulate the edge of the chip in a clockwise motion. Once you begin heating any motherboard, it is important to keep it Level and Stable.

Using the infrared Thermometer will take you a little bit of practice, as if it is used wrong it will yield misleading results… which could end up in overheating the Chipset if not getting the correct readings.

These Infrared thermometers are laser guided... You simply point the red dot to the spot you are testing for temperature readings. You should be holding the gun at a 45 degree angle and about 4 to 6 inches from the chip to get the correct readings... You do not exceed 223 degrees Celsius for the GPU heating.

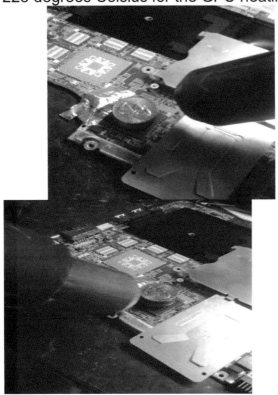

Now Comes the Heating of the Chip

Turn Your Heat Gun On Low...
Start at about 4 inches From the Chip...
You want to be holding the gun at a 45% angle...
Aim the heat at the Edge of the chip, You Will Start
Rotating around the Chip- around the outer edge of

the chip...then use tighter circles concentrating on the quarter stack, then after about 30-40 seconds, slowly move closer to the chip...You Want to Heat the Chip slowly... This Will At The Same Time Pre-Bake The Underside Of The Board...

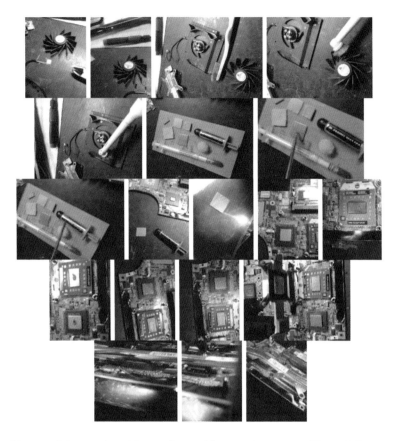

Never Move the Heat Gun Closer than the Top Of
Your Coin Stack...Then Pull It Back And Slowly
Repeat... The Chip Needs To Get Hot Enough
To Re-Melt the Solder Balls on the underside of the
graphics chip back down to the contact pads on the
Motherboard... and this takes Quite
A lot of heating to do.... You Must Not OVERHEAT
the Chip... It Is Best To Under heat it and have to
Redo... than to overheat... It will cause
The solder to break down and even crack/split...
causing failure forever...

This process will take about 3 minutes total... Once you shut off the Heat Gun... Leave The Stack of Coins on the Chip and Let Sit for another 5 minutes...
It is important to not take the heat above 433 F or 223 C

This is where a digital temperature probe comes in handy...If one is available to you, or you can purchase one... You will have better results
Now If you have a lot Of Repair Experience and Are Capable... You Can Go One Step Further And DO A Re-ball... You Would Be Completely Removing The Graphics Chip And Using Solder Wick To Clean The Contact Points On Both The Chip And The Motherboard. If Doing This, I recommend CHIP QUIK SMD REMOVAL KIT
Then Re-Balling Both The Chip And The Motherboard...To Do This, You Need To Add New Solder Balls To Each Contact Pad On The Chip And To The Motherboard.
You Would Also Need To Remove the Epoxy That the Factory Uses To Secure the Chip
The Process Once Again, A Little More Detailed...
And now it is time to start your heat gun... You should be using 600 to 800 degrees Fahrenheit temperature... Or if you have a 2 setting heat gun, then use the LOW setting...

Now you will add a Coin Stack to the top of the GPU on the Video Card... You will be Using 6 Quarters, And 2 Nickels

All U.S. nickels weigh 5 gm.

A Modern copper-nickel quarter dated 1965 and later will weigh 5.67 grams

You Place the 2 Nickels On the Chip First... This is because the Nickel is closer to the same size as the upper chip, being that the quarters are larger and higher up from the chips surface, will help pull the Heat away quicker and will heat the chip more thoroughly...

And now comes the Reflowing of the BGA GPU. If you don't have use of an infrared thermometer, you will have to judge your reflow by length of time...

Starting Your Reflow...

You start By Aiming your Heat Gun and turning it on, Hold at 45 degree angle, it's a Good Idea to Use a Stopwatch too... Type: STOPWATCH into Google and Run a Free One On Your Screen While Reflowing...

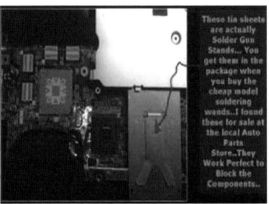

These tin sheets are actually Solder Gun Stands... You get them in the package when you buy the cheap model soldering wands...I found these for sale at the local Auto Parts Store..They Work Perfect to Block the Components..

PREPPING THE MOTHERBOARD

As you can see in the Above Photos, You are only going to be covering the components in the immediate area of the graphics chip..
There is NO need to wrap your motherboard up like a christmas present ...Just the components in the Immediate area...

Be Careful of the tiny capacitor in that spot... it's quite fragile and if not careful it can fall off it's pad and you won't even know it...

OK, As Soon as You Start Heating the Chip, You Will Be Aiming the Heat Gun around the Outer Edge of the Chip-.And The Base of the Coin Stack....
At The 1 Minute Point of Heating... Look At Your Digital Thermometer... You Should Be At A Temperature Of 160 Degrees Celsius...Then At The 2 minute point of reflowing... you should be at a temperature of 195 degrees Celsius....Then... at around 2:45 or 3 minutes... you should reach 223 degrees Celsius... the Reflow Point... The Point at Which The BGA Solder Turns To A Liquid State... And The Cracks/Faults In the Cold Solder BGA Should Reconnect/Recorrect.... In Turn, Repairing the Chip...

Once you have reached the correct temperature or time length... let the coin stack sit on top of the chip until cooled... then remove the coin stack and tin sheets/foil...

Now, when applying silver paste to the chip, you do not put a "ton" of it on... You will apply a thin layer of paste to the chip, and then, most importantly, you will then smooth the paste onto the chip... you spread it like making a peanut butter and jelly sandwich... make it Smooth! You don't want pits and dips in the paste... you want it looking like a Frosted Cake...

If your GPU had a thermal pad and didn't originally have thermal paste on it... then you will use a thermal pad again... whether it is the same pad as originally used, or a NEW replacement pad...It is important that a pad is used to allow for natural expansion/contraction of the fragile upper "flip" chip of the GPU..

And now you will put the Heatsink/Fan Assembly back onto the video chip/GPU or card.

Make sure to plug the fan back into its port on the card.

Now you are ready to test the card.

It would be a good idea to practice removal on a "dead" motherboard before attempting on the board you are repairing, unless you are familiar with the process and have done it more than a couple times... Main thing here is to go slow and do not overheat the chip doing it… Heat one side at a time... then gently scrape that one side… then heat the next side, then scrape and so on…

The Coin Stack – Used in the Reflow Process, A KEY INSTRUMENT IN VIDEO CHIP REPAIR
This is the key to a successful reflow, and the reason for my patent and trademark...

The coin stack plays several roles in the Reflow process... And Is the Reason why My Method Works and the "viral" YouTube Videos Do not...

I use a Coin stack because of the availability of a Coin world-wide... I started Out before Releasing this Method Using a Block of Silver, which equaled the weight of 6 Quarters and 2 Nickels... And since coins are easy for everyone World-Wide to obtain... I went with the common choice...

The Metal Compounds that make up these 2 coins will help greatly in the Dissipation of Heat.
The Importance of weighting the chip is my other main key reason for this method and its success...
It's a matter of the Laws of Science that anything being heated...especially to the temperature of a reflow.... will want to expand (as opposed to contracting)... and by nature... the chip will want to "expand" and rise up from its connection... This is also why Chip Sealant is used by the manufacturers...

So when heating the chip for a Reflow... Weighting this GPU chip will help to prevent chip rising and popcorning... Makes Sense Right?? Say "yes"....Cause It does... I have done extensive testing on this by using various weights and temperatures...
Now... the other purpose the coinstack serves is... It Protects the Chip
It protects it by covering the "flip chip" or Upper Chip... This is extremely important and was completely overlooked in any other Reflow process method I've come across...
The reason this is important is that when heating the graphics chip either in a Rework Station or by using a Heat gun... This Smaller Chip Is The First Chip Being

Exposed to The High Heat... And Being that it is a Smaller and Thinner chip... It is going to heat up to the point of reflow Way before the Lower Larger Chip Reaches the Proper Reflow Temperature...So that if No coin stack is used the Fully Exposed chip can possibly be irreversibly damaged before the lower chip reflow is complete...

The Coin Stack Prevents this from happening by its ability to Dissipate the heat rapidly from that upper chip during the heating process and not allowing direct heat to make contact ... Though this Flip Chip is allowed to still reach Reflow temperature at the same time as the Lower chip, Or not at all if desired... it is completely controllable now...The Coins will also Help In the Cooling Process, as they Will Pull the Heat from The Chip Much Quicker And Directly Instead of Dispersing it Downward through the Motherboard, which is Extremely Important.

External Video/GPU Card Repair

External Video/GPU Card Repair; Video cards are common in laptops and are removable:

Repairing the Laptops Video Card, Repairing the Desktops Video Card

REPAIRING A DESKTOP COMPUTER's VIDEO CARD

You Will Be Reflowing the GPU on the Card's board, The Repair Method Can Be Applied to ANY Video Card

This Video Card happened to have a "clean" fan...
Most will be loaded with dust and debris and will need
to be cleaned before repair completion.
Start the Repair by Unplugging the Fan/Heatsink
Assembly from the Board…

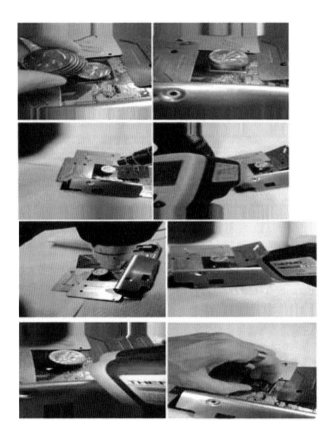

Desktop Video Card Failure is an extremely common
issue, to which the only "fix" has been to Throw out
the card and replace it with a new one...

Cards today can be quite costly...Costing up to $700.00(USD) and Higher...and to simply replace that expensive card is not an option for some people, and can render the computer Non-Working...

Most video card Failure Issues ARE related to Thermal Breakdown
A Desktop Video Card Has a Heat Sink and Fan for a Reason...it covers the GPU or Graphics /Video Chip to keep it cool. The GPU can fail when over exposed to extreme heat and internal case temperatures. The failure is usually due to the fan/heatsink assembly becoming clogged and hindering the full capability of the fan which in turn can cause faults in the BGA of the Graphics chip, causing the card to Not work, which causes the Desktop to Not Work and Not Able to POST.
The Same Method That Applies to Laptop Video Chip Repair, Applies also to Desktop Video Cards

Step 1 is to remove the Fan, Heatsink Assembly from the Video Card. To do this, you need to turn the video card to the opposite side of the fan (on most cards), and look for the Pin Clamps or Spring Screws... In the photos, the Plastic pop-thru and Lock type is used, and to remove, you will need to use a pair of needle nosed pliers and squeeze the 2 prongs together to be able to push the pins back through the holes...
Pull the Fan/Heatsink Assembly away from the video card and Set Aside.
At this time, you should Clean the Fan Blades, and the heatsink, Remove the Crusty Old Silver Thermal Paste and Replace with a SMOOTH Layer of New Silver Thermal Paste...

Next, it's time to Insulate the surrounding components on the video card to keep them cool during the reflow process... It is not necessary to Completely Wrap the card like a Christmas present with tin foil...
And now it is time to start your heat gun... You should be using 600 to 800 degrees Fahrenheit temperature... Or if you have a 2 setting heat gun, then use the LOW setting...

Now you will add a Coin Stack to the top of the GPU on the Video Card... You will be Using 6 Quarters, And 2 Nickels
All U.S. nickels weigh 5 gm.
A Modern copper-nickel quarter dated 1965 and later will weigh 5.67 grams
You Place the 2 Nickels On the Chip First... This is because the Nickel is closer to the same size as the upper chip, being that the quarters are larger and higher up from the chips surface, will help pull the Heat away quicker and will heat the chip more thoroughly...

And now comes the Reflowing of the BGA GPU. If you don't have use of an infrared thermometer, you will have to judge your reflow by length of time... Starting Your Reflow...
You start By Aiming your Heat Gun and turning it on, Hold at 45 degree angle, it's a Good Idea to Use a Stopwatch too... Type: STOPWATCH into Google and Run a Free One On Your Screen While Reflowing...
OK, As Soon as You Start Heating the Chip, You Will Be Aiming the Heat Gun around the Outer Edge of the Chip-.And The Base of the Coin Stack....
At The 1 Minute Point of Heating... Look At Your Digital Thermometer... You Should Be At A Temperature Of 160 Degrees Celsius...Then At The 2

minute point of reflowing... you should be at a temperature of 195 degrees Celsius....Then... at around 2:45 or 3 minutes... you should reach 223 degrees Celsius... the Reflow Point... The Point at Which The BGA Solder Turns To A Liquid State... And The Cracks/Faults In the Cold Solder BGA Should Reconnect/Recorrect.... In Turn, Repairing the Chip...

Once you have reached the correct temperature or time length... let the coin stack sit on top of the chip until cooled... then remove the coin stack and tin sheets/foil...

Now.... When applying silver paste to the chip, you do not put a "ton" of it on... You will apply a thin layer of paste to the chip, and then, most importantly, you will then smooth the paste onto the chip... you spread it like making a peanut butter and jelly sandwich... make it Smooth! You don't want pits and dips in the paste... you want it looking like a Frosted Cake... If your GPU had a thermal pad and didn't originally have thermal paste on it... then you will use a thermal pad again... whether it is the same pad as originally used, or a NEW replacement pad...It is important that a pad is used to allow for natural expansion/contraction of the fragile upper "flip" chip of the GPU..

And now you will put the Heatsink/Fan Assembly back onto the video card.

Make sure to plug the fan back into its port on the card. Now you are ready to test the card.

The Heat Gun in the photo above is a digital and adjustable
setting gun, the heat gun is set at 700 for Reflowing.

Nvidia Chipset will be the most common GPU/Video Chip that
you will be reflowing.

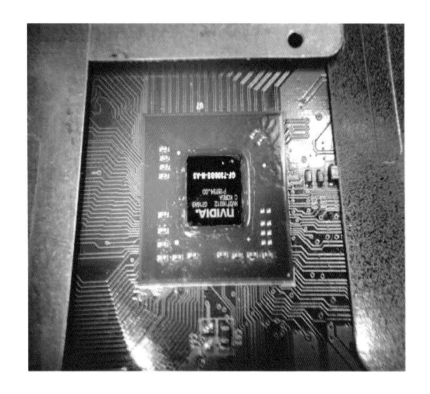

A VIEW OF THE GPU

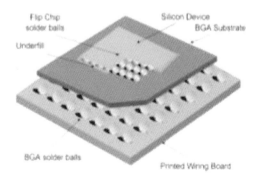

Flip Chip solder balls

Silicon Device

BGA Substrate

Underfill

BGA solder balls

Printed Wiring Board

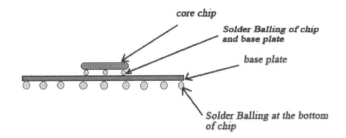

core chip

Solder Balling of chip
and base plate

base plate

Solder Balling at the bottom
of chip

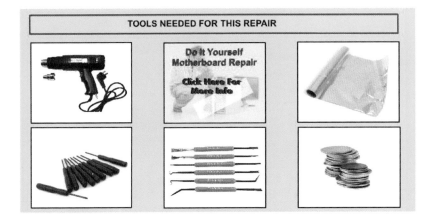

TOOLS NEEDED FOR THIS REPAIR

Do It Yourself
Motherboard Repair

Click Here For
More Info

I Use Metal And Aluminum Foil, I also Work On A Marble Table, You Will Want To Make Sure That You Have Foil Or Non Flamable Surface Under The Motherboard. The More You Cover.. The Better

It Is Important To Clear Your Work Area Now.. You Will Be Working With Alot Of Heat And Anything Around Will Get Real Hot

CLOSE UP VIEW OF THE COINSTACK

PHOTOS OF THE PROCESS

THE GPU (video chip, southbridge, graphics, integrated chipset)

**Notice the Red Chip sealant
applied around the outer edge
of the GPU, you will be removing
this, instructions are in this
book to do so.**

Covering the DIMM slots,
Removal of the RAM and CPU

Insulating the Components and Plastic Parts connected to the Motherboard

The Insulating Of The Motherboard

Placing The Smaller Of the
Coins On The Upper Flip Chip

Adding the 6 Quarters on top of the 2 Nickels

At this stage you can preheat the board to 140 degrees celcius and then apply a small amount of liquid No Residue

flux around the outer edge of the GPU, then continue to heat to 223 degrees and the liquid flux will flow into the underside of the chipset.

Heat the Chip on a 45 degree angle – 2-3 inches away

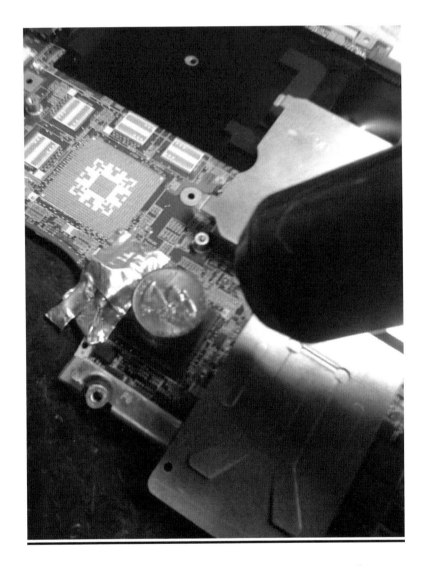

Aiming the heatsource at the edge of the chip and the coinstack

CLEANING THE FAN AND HEATSINK ASSEMBLY BEFORE REASSEMBLY IS EXTREMELY IMOPORTANT!

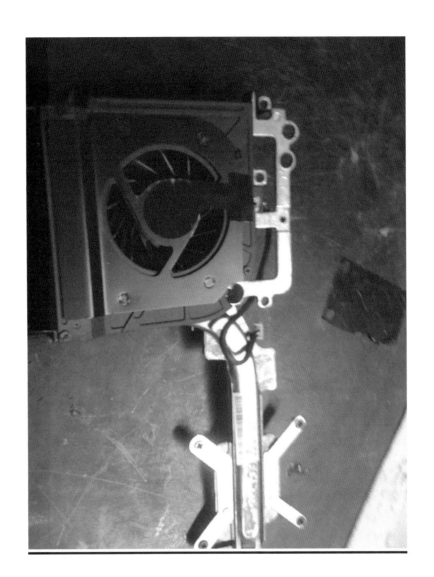

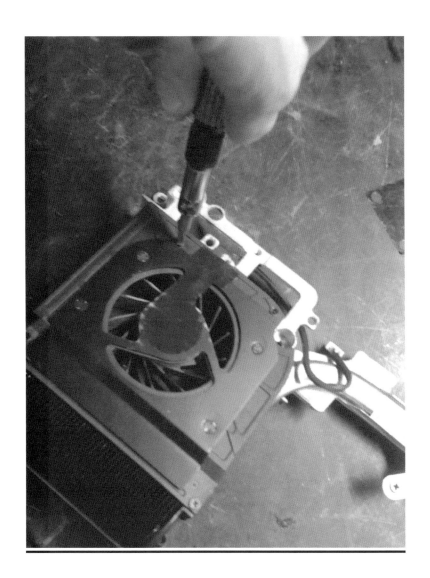

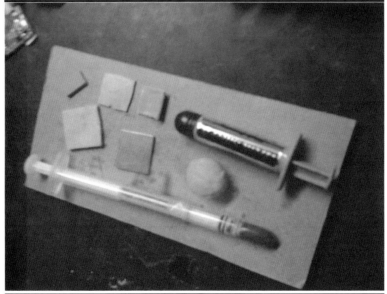

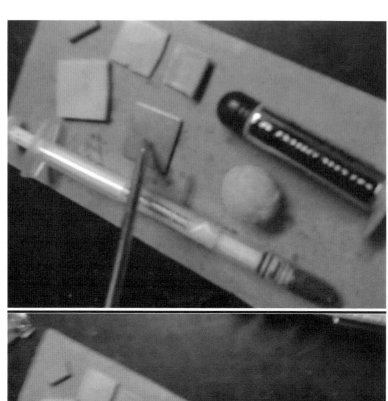

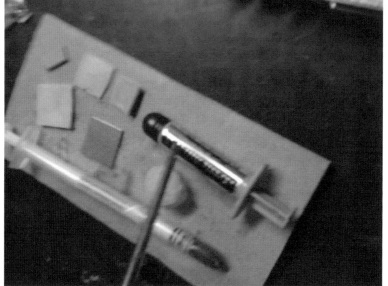

USING A COPPER SHIM (do not use a shim on a GPU that came from factory with a thermal pad)

You apply a thin layer of silver thermal paste to the shim (both sides) and the CPU, smooth it out, then re-apply the heatsink.

TIN SHEETS or Aluminum Foil is used to Insulate the motherboard components and fragile parts.

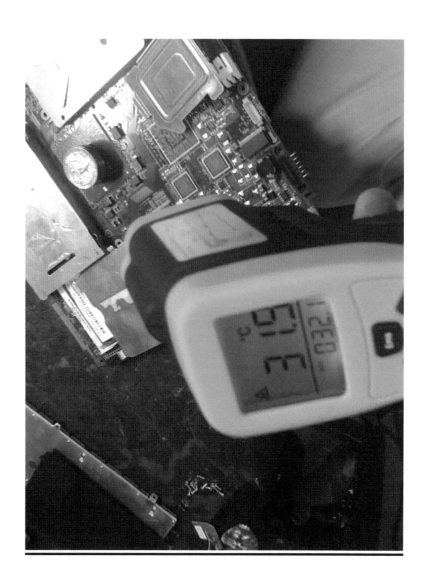

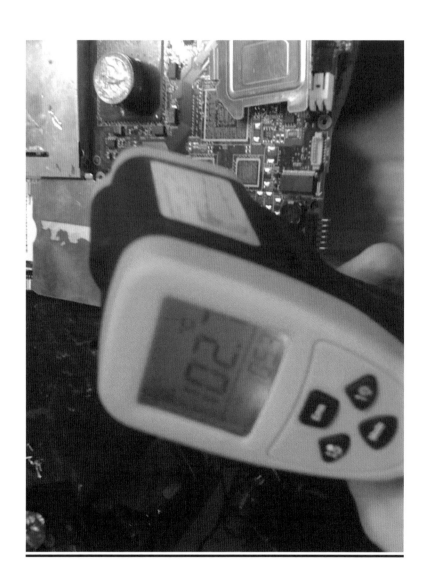

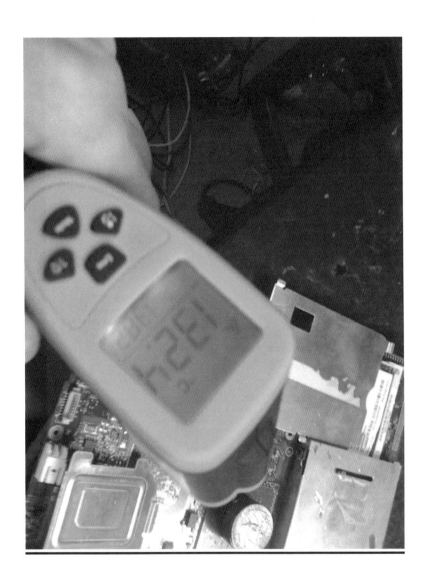

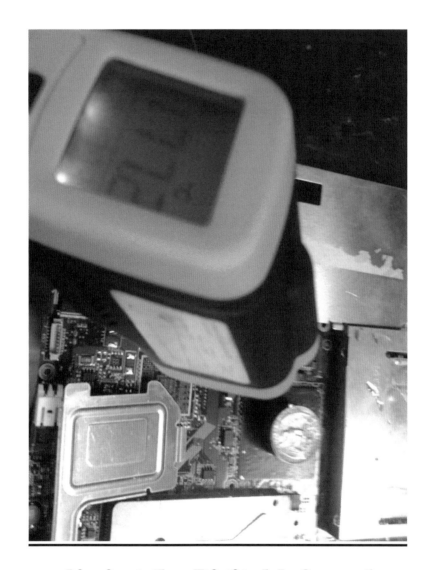

Aiming the Digital Infrared Thermometer

When 223 Degrees Celcius is reached, Hold for 2 to 3 seconds at a steady 223, then pull heat away from chip and let cool. Do not help the cooling in any way, let the chip cool at normal room temperature and at it's own pace. Cooling the chip too slow or too quick will cause New faults and cracks in the BGA.

Printed in Great Britain
by Amazon

77846707R00045